PAST and PRESENT

No 40

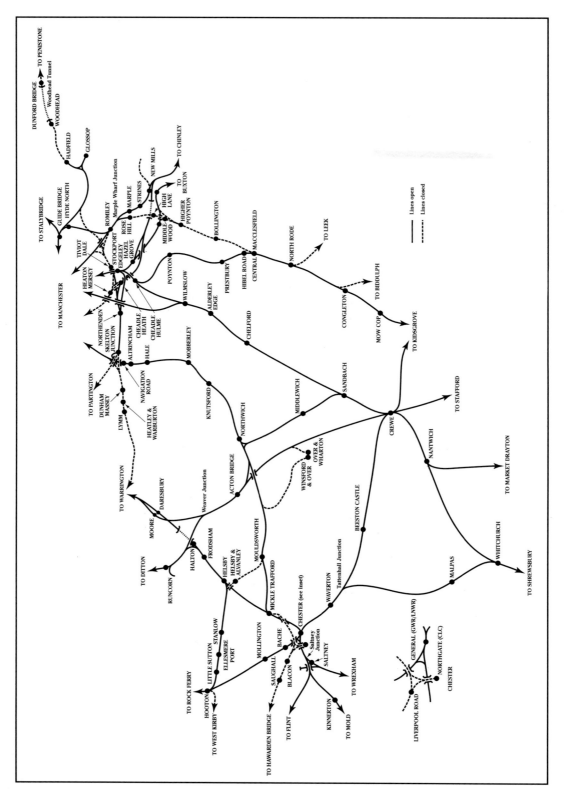

Map of the area covered by this book.

BRITISH RAILWAYS

PAST and PRESENT

No 40
Cheshire

Paul Shannon & John Hillmer

Past and Present

Past & Present Publishing Ltd

This book is dedicated to
the late Jim Peden

First published in 2003

British Library Cataloguing in Publication Data

A catalogue record for this book is available from the British Library.

ISBN 1 85895 232 8

Past & Present Publishing Ltd
The Trundle
Ringstead Road
Great Addington
Kettering
Northants NN14 4BW

Tel/Fax: 01536 330588
email: sales@nostalgiacollection.com
Website: www.nostalgiacollection.com

Printed and bound in Great Britain

FRODSHAM: To the east of Frodsham station two bridges cross first the River Weaver, then the Weaver Navigation. In 1966 a WD 'Austerity' 2-8-0 crosses the Weaver Navigation with oil empties for Stanlow. Already the bridge carries the pipeline from Stanlow to Heysham, which will contribute to the gradual loss of rail-borne petroleum traffic from Stanlow.

In the 'present' picture, taken on 28 March 2002, a two-car Class 158 is seen with the 0717 Manchester Piccadilly to Llandudno service. The only freight workings routed via Frodsham in the summer of 2002 were the daily trip working between Warrington and Dee Marsh Junction for Shotton Paper and timber trains between Warrington and Chirk. *John Feild/PDS*

CONTENTS

CHESTER GENERAL: The frontage of Chester General station has changed remarkably little since its opening as a joint venture by the Shrewsbury & Chester Railway and the Chester & Holyhead Railway in August 1848. In the first of these two views, taken in 1973, the station sports its British Railways 'lion and wheel' emblem and prominent nameboard in London Midland Region maroon. The suffix 'General' had become redundant with the closure of Northgate in 1969. The bus is a Guy Arab IV built in 1961; it remained in service with Chester City Transport until 1976.

The 'present' photograph, dated 20 January 2002, shows the station frontage now devoid of any nameboard but identified by the former BR 'double arrow' symbol – one of the few instantly recognisable national labels on today's fragmented railway system. Behind the façade the station concourse has received a major facelift, including a new travel centre. *John Feild/PDS*

INTRODUCTION

For a predominantly rural county, Cheshire once boasted a well-developed railway network with plenty of variety in terms of traction, traffic and railway architecture. Today, many of the lesser-used branch lines have gone, as has much of the freight in the county, but there have also been some positive developments such as the extension of third-rail electrification to Chester and Ellesmere Port, and the opening of the Manchester Airport branch.

In the pre-Grouping era, the London & North Western Railway was the most prominent main-line operator in Cheshire, its routes radiating from the railway town of Crewe to Chester, Liverpool, Warrington and Manchester. The LNWR also served Macclesfield and operated a number of secondary routes such as Skelton Junction to Warrington and Tattenhall Junction to Whitchurch.

Crewe itself needs little introduction as one of the nation's archetypal railway towns. Before the coming of the railway it was just a small agricultural village, but after the opening of lines to Chester and Manchester in the 1840s it became an important junction, and before long its rapidly expanding railway workshops made it one of the biggest locomotive construction centres in the country. The LNWR even provided Crewe with its essential community services such as water and gas supplies.

In the west of the county the Great Western Railway had an important influence, with its through expresses from London Paddington to Birkenhead via Chester. The company at one time even ran through coaches to Liverpool via the Mersey Railway tunnel. Despite their uneasy relationship with each other, the GWR and LNWR shared the operation of various lines to the north of Chester, under the title of the Birkenhead Joint Railway.

An unusual railway operator that survived as a separate entity until Nationalisation was the Cheshire Lines Committee, a tripartite alliance between the Manchester Sheffield & Lincolnshire Railway (which later became the Great Central Railway), the Great Northern Railway and the Midland Railway. Although many of its lines were actually in south Lancashire, the CLC network eventually spread right across the county from Godley Junction in the east to Chester Northgate in the west.

Smaller pre-Grouping presences in the county included the Great Central Railway, with its lines from Manchester to Sheffield via Penistone and from Chester to Hawarden Bridge, the Midland Railway, with its main line from Manchester Central to Chinley, and the Manchester South Junction & Altrincham Railway, which, as its name suggests, ran between Manchester and Altrincham. The lines through Romiley in the east of the county were run jointly by the GCR and MR.

Upon the 1923 Grouping, most lines other than those of the CLC became part of the London Midland & Scottish Railway. However, the GCR lines went to the London & North Eastern Railway – giving the LNER its only entry into Wales – and of course the GWR remained the GWR. So there was still plenty of variety in the county's railway operations, even if the fierce inter-company rivalry that had prevented a sensible connection from being commissioned at Mickle Trafford in the 1870s was now largely consigned to the past. Chester was remarkable after 1923 in having sheds belonging to three of the 'Big Four'; only the Southern Railway was not represented.

In the 1950s the British Railways regions continued to operate on similar lines to the post-Grouping companies, both in terms of service patterns and locomotive usage. Perhaps the most noticeable change in traction policy was the replacement of old GCR locomotives by newer LMS and BR standard types on lines formerly operated by the GCR and CLC.

Early passenger line closures included the Chester to Whitchurch service in 1957, the

STANLOW: The track layout at Stanlow was extensively remodelled from 1948 onwards to cope with rapidly increasing traffic from the Shell refinery complex. Backing its train of empties into the east end of the reception sidings in 1966 is ex-LMS '8F' 2-8-0 No 48365. At that time there were scheduled block oil trains from Stanlow to Barnsley Junction, Colwick, Etruria, Guide Bridge, Leeds, Morton, Uttoxeter and Whittington, together with trip workings to Ellesmere Port and Hooton.

By the date of the 'present' photograph, 14 February 2002, the Shell sidings had been cleared of tank wagons, but the track layout was still intact. However, any hopes of a rail freight revival here are faint. *John Feild/PDS (with thanks to Shell Research Limited)*

Middlewich line in 1960, and the Stockport to Warrington service in 1962. Meanwhile the 1955 Modernisation Plan brought the promise of 25kV electrification to the West Coast Main Line via Crewe, and freight carryings in the county were boosted by the expansion of the Shell refinery at Stanlow.

The Beeching Report of 1963 envisaged the closure of various rural routes, including the whole GCR system west of Chester, the Stockport Tiviot Dale to Glazebrook line, and the Macclesfield to Romiley line. It also proposed the closure of numerous small intermediate stations, especially those on the former LNWR main lines from Crewe to Chester, Liverpool and Warrington.

The measures proposed for rail freight in the Beeching Report were arguably more drastic than those proposed for the passenger network. Literally hundreds of poorly used station goods yards were to face closure across the BR network. There was to be a gradual shift from wagonload to trainload operation, with the introduction of liner trains where possible – the days of the pick-up goods train in Cheshire were numbered. Even Crewe was to lose its marshalling function to Warrington in 1972.

Although the recommendations of the Beeching Report in Cheshire were largely implemented, there were some notable exceptions. A number of threatened intermediate stations such as Frodsham, Helsby, Broadbottom and Newton (for Hyde) escaped the axe, while the Chester to Liverpool service via Runcorn hung on until 1975. On the other hand, the Woodhead route – which we have taken the liberty of including in this volume because of its considerable historical interest, even though it only skirted the 'pan-handle' of Cheshire – had a shorter future than Dr Beeching envisaged, with passenger services beyond Hadfield withdrawn in 1970.

One aspect of Dr Beeching's freight plans that never came to fruition was the proposed transfer of large quantities of wagonload traffic to liner trains. Several container depots were to be located on the fringe of Cheshire including Chester, Shrewsbury and Stoke-on-Trent. Interestingly, no terminal was proposed for Crewe, and the report made only a passing reference to the deep-sea business that in due course was to become the main source of rail-borne container traffic in Britain.

Changes in the last two decades of the 20th century included the gradual closure of most of the county's freight-only lines, with remaining services diverted over other routes where possible. Casualties included Godley Junction to Cheadle Junction in 1980, the Woodhead route beyond Hadfield in 1981, Skelton Junction to Warrington Arpley in 1985, the Over & Wharton branch in 1990, Helsby to Mouldsworth in 1991, and Mickle Trafford to Dee Marsh Junction in 1992. On a more positive note, passenger and freight lines in the Crewe area benefited from a major remodelling and resignalling exercise in 1985.

Much rail freight in the county has been lost since the 1970s, notably in the Stanlow and Ellesmere Port area, where several major customers including Shell, Kemira and Associated Octel all abandoned the use of rail. However, there have been some gains, such as the re-opening of the Runcorn Folly Lane branch in 2002 and the proposal to move large quantities of underground brine from Northwich by rail from 2003 onwards. The Basford Hall marshalling yard complex at Crewe remains busy, although its traffic profile has shifted considerably, with a reduction in container train marshalling balanced by growth in infrastructure traffic. The unusual 'independent lines' avoiding Crewe station continue to form an important freight corridor.

The passenger network as it stands today appears to be relatively stable. Investment in the last two decades has brought third-rail electrification to Chester and Ellesmere Port, the re-introduction of passenger services between Altrincham and Stockport – albeit only because of the conversion of the Altrincham to Manchester line for Metrolink services – and the opening of the Manchester Airport branch. New intermediate stations have included Runcorn East, Bache (replacing Upton-by-Chester), Overpool and Woodsmoor. For the future there has been talk of reviving the passenger service to Middlewich, although the necessary funding has yet to be identified.

Inevitably there is a depressing aspect to undertaking a 'past and present' comparison of

Cheshire's railways. Many of the pictures show decline of some kind or other, while those that show modernisation often involve the loss of interesting railway features such as signal boxes and intricate track layouts. Lineside photography has become more difficult too, partly due to the rapid growth of trees and bushes alongside most railway lines, and partly to the ugly spiked metal fencing that now flanks many routes.

Having said that, the experience of revisiting locations photographed 30 or 40 years ago is always exciting, especially so where there are still visible traces of a long-forgotten railway or station. We are conscious that the story is not finished yet. Many of the 'present' photographs included here will themselves become historic in the not too distant future, as Virgin 'Pendolinos' and 'Voyagers' take over InterCity services on the West Coast Main Line and as some of the older diesel types such as Class 56 are withdrawn from service.

Finally we must record our thanks to the many photographers and holders of photographic collections who made it possible to put this volume together. We are also grateful to Bryan Wilson, John Feild and David Rapson for providing valuable caption information.

John Hillmer, Wilmslow
Paul Shannon, Chester

BIBLIOGRAPHY

ABC British Railways Locomotives, combined volume 1953 (Ian Allan)

ABC Railway Freight Operations *by Paul Shannon* (Ian Allan)

BR Steam Motive Power Depots: LMR *by Paul Bolger* (Ian Allan)

BR Track Diagrams: No 4 London Midland Region (Quail Map Co)

The Cheshire Lines Committee *by Paul Bolger* (Heyday Publishing Company)

Cheshire Railways in Old Photographs *by Mike Hitches* (Alan Sutton Publishing)

Complete British Railways Maps & Gazetteer 1839-1981 *by C. J. Wignall* (OPC)

The Handbook of Steam Motive Power Depots (3) *by Paul Smith* (Platform 5)

Pennine Branch Lines *by Alan Earnshaw* (Ian Allan)

A Pictorial Survey of Railway Signalling *by D. Allen and C. J. Woolstenholmes* (OPC)

Portrait of the Cheshire Lines Committee *by Nigel Dyckhoff* (Ian Allan)

Rail Centres: Crewe *by Rex Christiansen* (Ian Allan)

Railway Postcard Scenes of Cheshire *by John Ryan and Basil Jeuda* (Cheshire Libraries)

Railway Stations of Wirral *by the Merseyside Railway History Group* (Ian & Marilyn Boumphrey)

A Regional History of the Railways of Great Britain: Volume 10 The North West *by Geoffrey O. Holt* (David & Charles)

Regional Railway Centres: North West *by Rex Christiansen* (Ian Allan)

Back issues of:
Branch Line News
The Railway Observer
Railway Magazine
Railway World
Modern Railways
Rail

Chester: GWR and LNWR lines

KINNERTON: Serving a rural community straddling the Cheshire-Flintshire border, Kinnerton was a minor intermediate station on the LNWR Chester to Mold line. LNWR 2-4-2T No 6624 calls with a local service to Mold in the early years of the 20th century.

Goods facilities were withdrawn from Kinnerton as early as 1955, but passenger trains continued to call there until closure of the line in 1962. Since then, the highway authorities have realigned the road to bisect the station site, as pictured on 16 March 2002. Much of the railway alignment between Broughton and Kinnerton is still traceable. *John Ryan collection/PDS*

SALTNEY: Class 5 4-6-0 No 45394 approaches Saltney Junction with a westbound mixed goods train on a sunny spring afternoon in 1953. At that time there were four well-used tracks between Chester and Saltney: two for the ex-LNWR main line to Holyhead and two for the ex-GWR route to Shrewsbury. Saltney itself was a busy location for goods traffic, with a branch from the GWR line passing under the LNWR tracks to reach various sidings alongside the Dee.

Following track rationalisation schemes in the 1980s, the only railway infrastructure remaining at Saltney is the double-track main line to Holyhead, together with a single lead junction for Wrexham and Shrewsbury, behind the photographer in this 'present' scene dated 16 March 2002. *JCH/PDS*

MOLLINGTON: Steam survived on the Wirral until the mid-1960s, with Birkenhead shed retaining an allocation of BR Standard Class '9Fs' for heavy freight work. No 92107 approaches the site of Mollington station, between Hooton and Chester, with a southbound goods train on the afternoon of 23 August 1966. The station at Mollington had closed to passengers in 1960, but at the time of the photograph the goods yard was still in use as an oil terminal.

Third-rail electrification was extended from Hooton to Chester in 1993, allowing Class 507 and 508 units to provide a half-hourly service to and from Liverpool. Unit No 508138 forms the 1356 Moorfields to Chester service on 27 March 2002. Timetabled freight between Hooton and Chester finished in the late 1990s following the end of oil trains from Stanlow.
Roger Siviter/PDS

BACHE: Class 5 No 45308, allocated to Stoke shed (5D), heads south between Upton-by-Chester and Chester with cattle vans from Birkenhead on 21 July 1967. The platforms of Upton-by-Chester station are just visible in the distance.

Cattle traffic on BR ceased shortly after the date of the 'past' photograph, and Upton-by-Chester station closed in January 1984 in favour of the new, more conveniently situated halt at Bache. By a stroke of good fortune the northbound platform at Bache provides a vantage point in almost the same location as the 'past' photograph, as unit No 508141 arrives with the 1402 Moorfields to Chester service on 3 March 2002. The sign 'For Chester Zoo' refers to a bus connection from the nearby highway. *John Feild/PDS*

CHESTER BROOK LANE: Pick-up goods trains and shunting movements were so commonplace in the pre-Beeching era that they generally went unrecorded. Thankfully this everyday but fascinating scene looking north from Brook Lane bridge in the late 1950s was captured on film. An unidentified '8F' heads unusually tender-first towards Birkenhead with a mixed goods train from Mold Junction, while ex-GWR Collett 0-6-0PT No 4602 shunts wagons from the nearby goods yard. The LNWR bracket signal is about to be replaced by a standard British Railways gantry.

More than 40 years later parts of the track layout are still recognisable, although the loop on the left-hand side sees little use. The right-hand track forms a headshunt for Chester depot. Unit No 507031 nears its journey's end with the 1232 Moorfields to Chester service on 2 February 2002. The footbridge of Bache station is visible in the distance. *John Feild/PDS*

CHESTER No 5: Viewed from the ex-CLC railway overbridge, Class '9F' 2-10-0 No 92131 passes Chester No 5 signal box in the summer of 1966 with a trainload of empty oil tanks bound for Ellesmere Port or Stanlow. The locomotive looks typically unkempt for the era, with its smokebox-door numberplate missing. In the middle distance, from left to right, are Chester's ex-GWR goods shed, ex-GWR steam locomotive shed and 1957 diesel multiple unit shed. The tracks curving round to the right form Chester West loop, providing a direct route for goods trains between the Wirral and locations to the west and south of Chester.

Today the location is known as Chester North Junction. Chester West loop still diverges to the right, but is used only by occasional infrastructure trains and passenger specials. The site of the GWR steam shed houses one of the newest traction maintenance depots in the country, dedicated to the upkeep of Class 175 'Coradia' diesel units. Class 507 unit No 507031 forms the 1320 departure from Chester to Liverpool on 2 February 2002. *John Feild/PDS*

CHESTER GWR SHED: Although the GWR and LNWR shared a single passenger station in Chester, they had separate locomotive sheds and separate facilities for goods. The GWR shed was located just west of Hoole Lane bridge, adjacent to Chester No 4 signal box, which controlled the junction of lines to Holyhead and Birkenhead. This 1958 view shows the shed with some of its typical ex-GWR allocation of the time, including a Churchward 2-6-0 and a Hawksworth 'County' 4-6-0. The shed supplied motive power for London Paddington to Birkenhead expresses as well as local passenger and goods trains from Birkenhead.

Chester GWR shed was an early casualty of dieselisation, losing its steam allocation in 1960. The shed buildings were then adapted for use as a diesel multiple unit depot. Further change came in 1999, when the site was chosen for the new Alstom Traincare depot for Class 175 'Coradia' units. That £17.3 million facility is pictured on 31 August 2002, with a passing InterCity 125 unit barely visible behind a rapidly growing line of trees. Royal Mail now occupies the former railway land on the south side of the main line. *Roger Carpenter (courtesy Mike Hitches)/PDS*

CHESTER DMU DEPOT retained an allocation of first-generation units until the 1990s. A Derby Class 108 unit is pictured beside the former steam maintenance building on 18 April 1981, while a four-car formation headed by a Metropolitan-Cammell Class 101 unit approaches the station. Just visible behind Chester No 4 box is a rake of engineers' wagons stabled in the sidings adjacent to Chester West loop.

Chester No 4 box and its associated semaphore signals were swept away in the 1980s Chester resignalling scheme. The siding layout was altered for the new Alstom maintenance depot, with the small track machine shed now accessed from the Chester station direction. Unit No 507010 recedes with the 0720 service from Chester to Liverpool Lime Street on 27 March 2002. *JCH/PDS*

CHESTER GENERAL (1): When first opened in 1848, Chester General station consisted of a single long through platform with bays at each end. A separate island platform with further bays was added in 1890. The layout then remained basically unchanged until the 1960s, when the trackwork of the original bays was rationalised. This view, dated 19 September 1959, shows BR Standard 4-6-0 No 73033 about to depart from platform 6 – one of the original east-facing bays – with a service for Crewe, while an unidentified 'Black 5' 4-6-0 waits alongside platform 8, the southernmost bay platform.

Today the former bay platforms 6 and 7 have become platforms 2 and 1 respectively, the latter having no scheduled passenger services. The track serving the former platform 8 was removed – together with a number of sidings on the south side – to provide improved car park access. In the 'present' photograph, dated 3 March 2002, unit No 158759 waits to leave platform 2 with a Crewe service, while 'Pacer' No 142011 is stabled by platform 1.
H. C. Casserley/PDS

CHESTER GENERAL (2): This fine 17 October 1966 study of Class '5MT' 2-6-0 'Crab' No 42942, allocated to Birkenhead (8H), waiting for a clear road towards Birkenhead recalls the days when Chester was alive with the sights and sounds of steam, with frequent shunting and run-round movements adding variety to the regular procession of main-line trains. However, in reality dieselisation was well advanced by this time, and No 42942 had only a few weeks left in service before withdrawal in January 1967.

Today, even diesel locomotives are a relatively infrequent occurrence at Chester, with most passenger trains formed by units of one kind or another. 'Coradia' unit No 175001 rolls into the station with the 1152 Holyhead to Crewe train on 27 March 2002. *Roger Siviter/PDS*

CHESTER GENERAL (3): Chester's two long through platforms provided excellent vantage points for observing railway activity around the station and adjacent goods sidings. 'Crab' No 42942 is seen again on the same day, this time on one of the through roads. Behind the locomotive smokebox is the long, partly covered footbridge that once provided direct passenger access between the station and Hoole Road.

The removal of the footbridge and of the left-hand building with the two chimneys has revealed the former LNWR goods warehouse, long since disconnected from the railway. Class 508 unit No 508125 arrives on Chester's only electrified platform line with the 1426 service from Moorfields on 31 March 2002. *Roger Siviter/PDS*

CHESTER GENERAL (4): 'Black Five' No 45238 passes Chester station on the up through line with a van train bound for the Crewe direction on 22 August 1966. Parcels trains in the 1960s and 1970s were notable for producing varied mixtures of rolling-stock: this formation includes ex-SR, ex-LMR and ex-GWR vehicles as well as BR standard stock.

The two through lines at Chester General were replaced by a single bi-directional line during the 1980s resignalling scheme. Part of the canopy over the main island platform has disappeared, as has the footbridge. A four-car combination of units Nos 158750 and 156466 departs with the 1258 Bangor to Crewe service on 3 March 2002, while a Class 175 'Coradia' unit waits in the adjacent bay platform. The decline of parcels traffic on Britain's railways has been even more dramatic than that of freight. In 2002 Chester no longer sees any parcels or mail trains, the last service to and from Holyhead having been withdrawn in the 1990s. *Tom Heavyside/PDS*

CHESTER GENERAL (5): Chester's LNWR-style lower-quadrant semaphore signals were gradually replaced by BR standard upper-quadrants, until they too were superseded by multiple-aspect colour lights in the 1980s. An LNWR bracket with two lower-quadrant arms is flanked by two BR standard brackets at the east end of the station in this view dated 29 January 1977. Arriving from the Crewe direction is a four-car DMU with a Metropolitan-Cammell twin set leading.

No trace remains today of the imposing Chester No 2 signal box, and the track layout has been simplified – probably a little too much in view of the increased number of passenger trains now using the station. Unit No 158757 arrives with the 1617 Manchester Piccadilly to Llandudno service on 8 May 2002; it will use the crossover half way along the station to call at the west end of platform 3. *JCH/PDS*

CHESTER No 2: This fine 1960s picture of the east end of Chester station recalls the dominance of wagonload freight operations in the pre-Beeching era. The ex-LNWR goods depot on the right is busy with 10-foot-wheelbase vans of various origins, each with a nominal capacity of just 12 tonnes and in practice probably carrying even less than that. 'Patriot' 4-6-0 No 45547 is shunting a Conflat wagon loaded with an A-type 'door to door' container

sandwiched between two BR standard parcels vehicles – a BG and a CCT – which would have been quite modern at the time of the photograph. Chester No 2 box had a 182-lever LNWR frame and controlled a short but busy section of track.

Chester No 2 box was closed on 6 May 1984, two days after the commissioning of Chester power signal box. Negotiating the much simplified track layout on 25 June 1999 is Rail Express Systems-liveried Class 47 No 47787 with the 5F95 empty mail vans from London Euston to Warrington. This train had been diverted via Chester following an accident at Winsford on the West Coast Main Line and a derailment on the usual alternative route via Middlewich. *Peter Owen collection/PDS*

24

CHESTER No 1 signal box marked the divergence of lines to Warrington and Crewe. Unlike most of the Chester boxes, it was a relatively modern BR structure. Recalling the days of well-loaded locomotive-hauled trains carrying holidaymakers to and from the North Wales coast, Class 40 No 225 takes the Warrington line on departing from Chester on 7 July 1973. This locomotive became No 40025 in the 1976 TOPS renumbering scheme and was withdrawn from Longsight depot in 1982.

The 1980s preference for single-lead junctions is all too evident in the 'present' view of Chester East Junction dated 27 March 2002. Unit No 158753 takes the Crewe line with the 1127 Bangor to Birmingham New Street service. *Tom Heavyside/PDS*

CHESTER LNWR SHED (1): The LNWR was the dominant pre-Grouping railway company in Chester, with its main lines radiating to Crewe, Warrington and Holyhead. The company built its locomotive shed in the fork of the Crewe and Warrington routes, about half a mile east of General station. Pictured outside the shed in the early 1920s is LNWR 'Large Jumbo' 2-4-0 No 2186 *Lowther*, built in 1896.

The career of *Lowther* came to an end in 1927, but the shed retained a varied allocation of steam locomotives until its closure in 1967. Today the road overbridge and houses remain, as do the (out of sight) railway routes to Crewe and Warrington, while the west end of the shed site has become the perfect playground for fledgling trainspotters, as pictured on 27 October 2001. *John Feild collection/PDS*

CHESTER LNWR SHED (2): In its later years Chester LNWR shed was home to various classes of freight and mixed traffic engines. This 1967 view looking towards Crewe shows the shed just a few weeks before its closure, with two 'Black Fives' and a 'Jinty' on the coaling line and further 'Black Fives' on shed.

Most of the land formerly occupied by the shed is now a housing estate, and it is hard to believe that there were ever sidings here. Class 175 'Coradia' unit No 175011 slows down for the approach to Chester station on 15 May 2002, forming the 1423 from Birmingham New Street to Holyhead. *John Feild/PDS*

WAVERTON: Ex-LMS '8F' 2-8-0 No 48225 passes Waverton on the Chester to Crewe line with an up partially fitted goods train on 17 October 1966. By this time all intermediate passenger stations between Chester and Crewe had closed, but the line still saw a wide variety of traction on through passenger and goods workings. No 48225 was a visitor from Kirkby-in-Ashfield (16C) in Nottinghamshire, but the class was a familiar sight on most of the ex-LMS network.

By 2002 freight traffic on the Chester to Crewe line had dwindled to between zero and two return workings each weekday. The monotony of diesel units was, however, still broken by regular Virgin Class 47 passenger duties between Crewe and Holyhead. No 47854 heads the 0919 Holyhead to London Euston train past Waverton on 27 March 2002. This working went over to InterCity 125 operation in September 2002. *Roger Siviter/PDS*

MALPAS: The LNWR cross-country line from Tattenhall Junction (on the Chester to Crewe line) to Whitchurch never realised its potential to compete with the GWR route for traffic between Chester and Shrewsbury. The principal intermediate station was Malpas, but even that was situated well away from the village centre and cannot have generated a huge volume of traffic. The Chester-bound platform is pictured from a passing train on 26 August 1954.

Malpas closed to passengers in 1957 but goods traffic continued until the complete closure of the line in 1963. Since then the station building has been restored and converted into offices, as pictured on 27 March 2002. *R. M. Casserley/PDS*

Chester: CLC and GCR lines

MOULDSWORTH: The first railway route through Mouldsworth was the CLC line from Northwich to Helsby & Alvanley, opened to goods in 1869 and to passengers in 1870. A connection with the Birkenhead Joint Railway at Helsby (West Cheshire Junction) followed in 1871, giving the CLC access to the Wirral and Ellesmere Port. Mouldsworth then became a junction with the completion of the CLC branch to Chester Northgate in 1874. Before long the Chester route became the main line, as least as far as passenger services were concerned. However, the Helsby & Alvanley route remained busy with goods traffic to and from the developing chemical industries around Ellesmere Port. In this 1966 photograph the Mouldsworth signalman waits to receive the single-line token as '9F' 2-10-0 No 92020 comes off the Helsby & Alvanley line with a Birkenhead to Northwich block working. The two tracks of the branch converged into one just round the corner.

A return visit to Mouldsworth on 14 February 2002 found the 1894-built signal box still in use and the pointwork still in situ. Even a rural location such as this has sprouted spiked metal fencing – one of the less attractive but characteristic features of Britain's railways at the turn of the 21st century. 'Sprinter' unit No 150144 approaches the station with the 1357 First North Western service from Chester to Manchester Piccadilly. *John Feild/PDS*

MICKLE TRAFFORD: The railway geography at Mickle Trafford, with the CLC line running beside the Birkenhead Joint line for a short distance before crossing over it, shows clearly how the early railway builders intended to link their systems together. However, the two pre-Grouping companies were unable to reach a satisfactory agreement and it was not until 1942 that the Government finally paid for an emergency connection, enabling through running from Warrington and Helsby to Chester Northgate and the Wirral via Dee Marsh Junction. Mickle Trafford itself once had two adjacent stations; both were closed to passengers in 1951, although the goods yard on the CLC route lasted until 1963. The goods shed was still standing in 1966 when an unidentified Class '9F' was caught on camera with a rake of 21-ton mineral wagons from the Chester Northgate direction.

The track layout at Mickle Trafford was altered in 1969 to allow trains from Northwich to run over ex-Birkenhead Joint metals to Chester General. The line from Mickle Trafford to Dee Marsh Junction then became freight-only, before closing completely in 1992. Today the CLC goods shed still stands, although all other traces of the yard have disappeared.

The third picture shows the BR signal box at Mickle Trafford, opened in 1969 to control the remodelled junction. *John Feild/PDS (2)*

CHESTER NORTHGATE (1): Although eclipsed by the grander and busier Chester General station, the CLC terminus at Northgate added considerably to the variety of locomotives and rolling-stock to be seen in Chester. The CLC provided Northgate with an overall roof, spanning the two platform lines and two further tracks in the middle – one for standage and the other a run-round loop. A curious feature of Northgate was its supposedly temporary entrance located at the platform ends, used for many years in preference to the inconveniently situated permanent entrance further along the western platform. The exterior is pictured in 1959, when train services were still operating from Northgate to Wrexham and the Wirral as well as Manchester. The billboard advertising the cheap day return fare to Rhyl and Prestatyn is perhaps misleading, as these resorts were served only from Chester General.

After Northgate closed, this prime city centre site was redeveloped as the Northgate Arena sports complex. The entrance is pictured on 20 January 2002. *John Feild/PDS*

Ex-Great Central Railway 'Director' Class D11 4-4-0 No 62662 *Prince of Wales* has just arrived at Northgate's eastern platform after working the 9.48 service from Manchester Central on 12 October 1957. The 9E shed plate refers to Trafford Park. *John Feild*

CHESTER NORTHGATE (2): By the mid-1960s all scheduled services from Northgate were worked by diesel multiple units. The 'past' photograph, dated 1967, shows one of the last appearances of a steam engine at the decaying terminus: Ivatt 2-6-0 No 46512 is ready to depart with a special comprising brand-new BR Mark I coaches. By this time Northgate had closed to goods traffic and the eastern half of the train shed had disappeared, but the track layout in the station was still intact.

The same vantage point today overlooks the rear of the Northgate Arena. The only feature visible in both photographs is the tower block on the extreme left. *John Feild/PDS*

CHESTER NORTHGATE SHED (1): The CLC was unusual in not possessing its own locomotives. Instead, it used the motive power of one of its parent companies, the Manchester Sheffield & Lincolnshire Railway (later to become the Great Central Railway). However, the CLC did build its own engine sheds, including Chester Northgate, which opened in 1874 as a sub-shed of Northwich. The locomotive allocation at Northgate remained dominated by ex-Great Central types throughout the LNER era and into the 1950s. Class 'C13' 4-4-2T No 7400 – soon to become British Railways No 67400 – stands outside the two-road shed building on 24 April 1947.

The skyline chimney pots provide a tenuous link with the 'present' photograph, dated 20 January 2002. The spike-topped palisade fencing betrays the alignment of the Chester to Holyhead main line, which used to be crossed by the CLC tracks. *H. C. Casserley/PDS*

CHESTER NORTHGATE SHED (2): During the British Railways era Northgate shed gradually saw its ex-Great Central engines replaced by ex-LMS and BR Standard types. Pictured on the turntable in this late 1950s scene is ex-LMS 2-6-2T No 40110, allocated to Wrexham Rhosddu (84K) from 1957 until 1960 and regularly employed on the local passenger service between Wrexham and Chester Northgate. The line-up in the background comprises a BR Standard 2-6-0 flanked by two ex-LNER (Great Central Railway design) 'O4' 2-8-0s. The letter would have worked into Dee Marsh from either Manchester or Godley.

Chester Northgate and Wrexham Rhosddu sheds both closed in 1960, as steam on local passenger workings was replaced by diesel traction. The access road to the Northgate Village housing estate now crosses the site of the turntable, as pictured on 21 March 2002. *John Feild/PDS*

CHESTER LIVERPOOL ROAD: The Manchester Sheffield & Lincolnshire Railway (MSLR) opened its link from Chester Northgate to Hawarden Bridge in 1890, enabling trains from the CLC Northwich line to reach Wrexham without passing over rival Birkenhead Joint Railway metals. The MSLR built its own station at Chester Liverpool Road, but in practice most of its services used the Northgate terminus. Liverpool Road became just a minor intermediate calling point and, given its proximity to Northgate, was an obvious target for rationalisation. It closed to passengers and general goods traffic in 1951, but the disused platforms are still in situ on 3 September 1964 as 'Black Five' No 45004 comes off the Northgate avoiding line with 1Z51, a Cadburys special to Moreton.

'Total Fitness' occupies part of the former station site today, flanked by the popular cycleway and footpath to Hawarden Bridge. The 'present' view is dated 21 March 2002. *John Feild/PDS*

BLACON: The former MSLR line from Chester Northgate to Hawarden Bridge continued to support local services to both Wrexham and New Brighton until well into the BR era. Both routes were circuitous and much of the traffic was to and from the intermediate stations. The through journey from Chester to Wrexham via the GCR took around 50 minutes, compared with just 19 minutes non-stop via the ex-GWR line. A Derby lightweight unit calls at Blacon's neglected but serviceable Chester-bound platform with a New Brighton to Chester Northgate working in 1966. A Guy Arab double-decker, typical of Chester bus services at that time, crosses the station bridge.

The line through Blacon closed to passengers in 1968 and to freight in 1984. It re-opened in 1986 as a single-track freight-only line – mainly for trainloads of steel coil from Ravenscraig to Shotton – but closed for good in 1992 after the closure of Ravenscraig. In retrospect it seems surprising that the distinctive station building at Blacon was not saved and restored, as many others have been. The recently opened cycleway is pictured on 2 February 2002. *John Feild/PDS*

SAUGHALL was an early casualty of British Railways cutbacks, closing to both passengers and goods in 1954. It was surrounded mainly by fields, while the village of Saughall was better served by the next station along the line at Sealand. Class 'C13' 4-4-2T No 67433 arrives at Saughall with a Wrexham to Chester train in 1951.

Nearly half a century after closure, traces of the westbound platform at Saughall remain, as pictured on 2 February 2002. Public transport looked set to return to the railway corridor when during the late 1990s Cheshire and Flintshire County Councils proposed building a guided busway alongside the cycle path. However, in September 2002 Cheshire councillors voted against funding the scheme, not least because of its estimated price tag of £18 million. *Stations UK/PDS*

Hooton to Helsby

HOOTON is the starting point for the 8½-mile line to Helsby, opened by the Birkenhead Joint Railway in 1863 to provide a through route from Stockport to Birkenhead. About to depart from Hooton on 27 July 1966 is Standard '4MT' 2-6-0 No 76052, allocated to Chester shed, with a morning train from Birkenhead Woodside. This was the last full year of steam-hauled passenger trains through Hooton.

Third-rail electrification from the Wirral reached Hooton in 1985 and was extended to Chester in 1993. Today Hooton enjoys a 15-minute off-peak electric service from Liverpool, with trains continuing alternately to Chester and Ellesmere Port. A Class 508 unit carrying Arriva branding departs for Chester on 2 July 2002. *B. Taylor/JCH*

LITTLE SUTTON was one of the three intermediate stations between Hooton and Helsby dating back to the opening of the line. The station, with its substantial house on the eastbound platform, is pictured on 26 August 1960. The platform-mounted signal box controlled access to the goods yard, which remained open for coal traffic until the late 1960s.

Since BR extended electrification from Hooton to Ellesmere Port in 1994, Little Sutton has enjoyed its best ever train service, with a half-hourly off-peak frequency to and from Liverpool. Merseyrail unit No 508134 arrives with the 1047 service from Liverpool Moorfields on 9 March 2002. *H. C. Casserley/PDS*

ELLESMERE PORT station was known originally as Whitby Locks, a reference to the Shropshire Union Canal, which enters the Mersey at this point. Industry and port facilities quickly colonised the area and the station was renamed Ellesmere Port in 1870. It became the main focus of rail traffic on the Hooton to Helsby line, with a busy station goods yard and numerous private siding facilities. The 'past' photograph, looking east from Westminster bridge, appears to have been taken in the late 1950s.

Today Ellesmere Port is the meeting place for two terminating passenger services – electric from Liverpool via Hooton and diesel from Helsby. Goods traffic has been sparse since the closure of the Manchester Ship Canal lines to Eastham and Ellesmere Port Docks, but in 2001 trainloads of Vauxhall cars were using the Richard Lawson loading point just west of the station. Brake-van B955167 leads a rake of empty car carriers heading for the Richard Lawson sidings on 29 August 2001, with Class 66 No 66147 providing power from the rear.

The third photograph shows Ellesmere Port in the era of the diesel service between Helsby and Rock Ferry. A Metropolitan-Cammell unit formed of vehicles Nos M53208 and M54060 forms the 1658 departure from Helsby on 6 July 1983. The station still had a generous array of semaphore signals, and the goods yard, which closed to revenue-earning freight in 1970, was still in use for engineers' traffic. *Cheshire & Chester Archives and Local Studies/PDS (2)*

ELLESMERE PORT EAST: The heavy concentration of chemical and petroleum industries around Ellesmere Port necessitated the building of Ellesmere Port East sorting sidings, about half a mile east of the passenger station. These sidings remained busy throughout the 1980s, handling wagonload traffic for Birkenhead as well as locally generated flows of chemicals and oil. On 14 August 1986 pilot loco No 08927 shunts an assortment of wagons that have just arrived on 7T68, the 1300 Speedlink feeder service from Warrington Arpley. The traffic includes an empty tank for Associated Octel, another empty tank for the storage terminal at Eastham and an HEA hopper wagon with domestic coal for Birkenhead. Main-line locomotives of Classes 25, 47 and 56 are visible in the background.

The loss of freight traffic from the Ellesmere Port area in the 1990s was dramatic. Shell pulled out of rail altogether, apart from a single inward flow of propylene, the Manchester Ship Canal railway closed totally, and the yard became little more than a storage location for condemned wagons. Freightliner Class 66 No 66545 runs round its train of empty propylene tanks in the loop beside the yard on 13 March 2002, forming 6E40, the 1520 from Stanlow to Humber. This service had only recently been handed over from EWS to Freightliner, leaving EWS with no regular freight traffic in the Ellesmere Port area. *Both PDS*

STANLOW: From the late 1980s some Irish container traffic was routed via Ellesmere Port and carried on scheduled feeder services to and from Crewe Basford Hall yard. Railfreight Distribution-liveried Class 47 No 47289 passes Stanlow with 4K43, the 1419 departure from Ellesmere Port, on 10 August 1989. At this time the Shell loading racks on the left were busy with rail traffic and the Manchester Ship Canal line on the right was still in position, albeit little used.

The container traffic to Ellesmere Port lasted only a few years. A bigger blow for rail freight was the decision by Shell to close its rail loading facility with effect from March 1998. Freightliner locos Nos 66546 and 66605 pass the abandoned loading racks with 6E40, the 1520 Stanlow to Humber empty propylene tanks, on 2 September 2002. *Both PDS*

HELSBY (1): Before dieselisation, the Helsby to Hooton service employed push-pull stock powered by a BR Standard 2-6-2 tank engine. Waiting to form the 2.05pm departure from Helsby to Hooton on 10 October 1959 is push-pull coach W24442M, powered from the rear by Class 2MT 2-6-2T No 84000.

After electrification of the Hooton to Ellesmere Port section, the residual diesel service between Ellesmere Port and Helsby soon dwindled to just a handful of trains in the early morning and mid-afternoon, unlikely to be of much use to potential customers. Unit No 150137 waits to depart from Helsby with the 1548 service to Ellesmere Port on 13 March 2002. *H. C. Casserley/PDS*

HELSBY (2): The station was opened by the Birkenhead, Lancashire & Cheshire Junction Railway in 1852, two years after the line from Chester had been inaugurated. It became a junction in 1863 when the branch from Hooton opened, enabling trains between Birkenhead and Warrington to bypass Chester. In the postcard photograph taken around 1900, smoke obscures the rear of the train as it approaches the junction from the Chester direction, but the station layout can clearly be seen. The footbridge was covered at a later date, probably reflecting the increased number of passengers using the station.

Approximately 100 years later, the changes have been surprisingly few. In the 'present' view of 2 September 2002, the footbridge has lost its cover, the tall semaphore signals have been cut down and the five poplars have gone, as Class 158 No 158754 calls with the 0947 service from Llandudno to Manchester Piccadilly. A small housing estate has been built on the village side of the line and, although unmanned, the station is well cared for by local volunteers. There is an hourly service between Manchester and Chester/North Wales, although

only four trains a day run between Helsby and Ellesmere Port, but judging by the regularly full car park the station is well patronised. Following the loss of oil traffic from Stanlow there is very little freight traffic.

The third picture, taken on 27 March 2002, shows the well-preserved station building on platform 1. The North Cheshire Rail Users' Group does an excellent job of maintaining the facilities at Helsby and Frodsham stations, as well as campaigning for improved rail services. *Basil Jeuda collection/JCH/PDS*

HELSBY & ALVANLEY was the only intermediate passenger station on the West Cheshire extension line from Mouldsworth to Helsby (West Cheshire Junction). It led a quiet existence, handling mainly unadvertised workers' trains for the nearby British Insulated Cable Company factory, and finally closed in 1964. The BICC factory also had its own private sidings and produced substantial quantities of goods traffic. In this 1966 scene an unidentified (and unidentifiable!) Crosti '9F' heads towards Mouldsworth with a train of empty open wagons for Northwich.

The Helsby to Mouldsworth line remained busy with petroleum, chemicals and fertiliser traffic until the 1980s until a fire in West Cheshire Junction signal box precipitated its closure in 1991; however, given the run-down of rail freight around Ellesmere Port, it is doubtful that the line would have survived into the 21st century in any case. Part of the trackbed is now an unofficial footpath, as pictured on 24 March 2002. *John Feild/PDS*

Around Runcorn

FRODSHAM: Opened in 1850 by the Birkenhead, Lancashire & Cheshire Junction Railway, Frodsham is pictured in this postcard view dated circa 1907 with passengers waiting for a local train to Chester, while an eastbound service stands in the other platform. There were goods facilities on both sides of the lines.

Today the goods shed still stands, albeit in the middle of a car park, and the station building on the down side has changed very little, other than the loss of the canopy. Frodsham is served by the basically hourly service between Manchester and North Wales via Chester. Class 158 No 158757 forms a Chester-bound train on the bright sunny morning of 2 September 2002. *Basil Jeuda collection/JCH*

RUNCORN (1): The most important station on the line from Weaver Junction (on the WCML) to Liverpool Lime Street, Runcorn was opened by the LNWR in 1869. Situated just south of the River Mersey at the point where the river begins to open out into its estuary, the railway is carried across the water by an impressive bridge. On 10 October 1959 ex-LMS 4-6-2 No 46206 *Princess Marie Louise* heads the 8.15am Euston to Lime Street train.

In the 'present' picture the scene has not changed all that much. The electrification of the line brought the overhead wires and masts, the semaphore signal has been replaced by a colour light, and of course the water column has gone. A Class 220 'Voyager' is pulling away with a Plymouth to Liverpool Lime Street service on 6 August 2002. *H. C. Casserley/JCH*

RUNCORN (2): The view northwards on 10 October 1959 shows the station before the modernisation and electrification of the line, completed in 1962. The old station buildings and footbridge were soon to be swept away and replaced by modern structures.

In the 'present' picture Class 158 No 158782 stops with a Central Trains service from Birmingham New Street to Lime Street. The current timetable shows that all passenger trains stop at Runcorn in both directions, the principal operator being Virgin with its West Coast and Cross Country Trains. *H. C. Casserley/JCH*

HALTON: Situated on the line from Warrington Bank Quay to Chester, between Runcorn East and Frodsham, Halton station was known as Runcorn when it first opened in 1851. It later became Runcorn Road before finally adopting the name of Halton in 1869. It closed to passengers in 1952. In the 'past' picture, taken in the mid-1960s, the up platform remains in situ as ex-LMS Class 5 4-6-0 No 44761 heads west.

Today there is no visual evidence of the station. On 27 March 2002, Class 150 No 150134 forms the 1449 from Liverpool Lime Street to Ellesmere Port, the only daily through train on that route. *John Feild /PDS*

DARESBURY: Known as Moore until 1861, Daresbury station lay on the line from Chester, just south of its junction with the West Coast Main Line. The station closed to passengers in 1952. On 28 June 1967 '9F' 2-10-0 No 92023 passes Daresbury signal box with an oil train heading towards Warrington. Opposite the box were sidings following the alignment of the West Coast main line before it was diverted over the bridge across the Manchester Ship Canal.

Today there are still signs of the cutting on the left, although nature has largely taken over. Class 142 No 142063 is seen on a Manchester to Chester working on 2 September 2002. *Jim Peden/JCH*

Mid-Cheshire

ACTON BRIDGE (1): Looking south from the station footbridge on 31 May 1958, the crowded platform makes one wonder where the people have come from and where they are going – perhaps a railtour? A glance at the OS map will show how little population there is in the area around the station, and there would have been even less in 1958.

Today the signal box, platform canopy and the siding on the up side have all gone, as a new Virgin 'Voyager' Class 221 heads north on 6 August 2002. *John Ryan collection/JCH*

ACTON BRIDGE (2): In the view looking north on 27 April 1951 we can see a fairly substantial platform building on the down side, a low canopy on the island platform and a goods shed in front of the booking office on the up side.

Today the station has been modernised with small brick waiting shelters and no platform facilities. The booking office and entrance building remains, but is hidden by the trees. On 6 August 2002 a Virgin 'Voyager' speeds through with an up service. *H. C. Casserley/JCH*

ACTON BRIDGE (3): An ex-LMS 'Black 5' 4-6-0 hurries south at the head of a 1Z35 'special' with a 10 or 11-coach train in the mid-1960s. The photograph was taken close by the footbridge situated a couple of hundred yards south of the station. Note the spur and buffer stop at the end of the down loop in the foreground where it joins the down main, and also the extensive rodding.

Since the 1960s there has been considerable tree growth and the nearest position now is from the top of the footbridge looking down on the track towards the station. The cottages remain but are completely hidden in the 'present' picture of 6 August 2002, as a Virgin 'Voyager' speeds through the station. *K. Sanders/JCH*

NORTHWICH, WEST JUNCTION: At the west end of the triangle junction two Class 20s, Nos 20013 and 20031, are at the head of the 1315 Tunstead-Oakleigh loaded limestone train, reporting number 6F42, on 15 September 1984.

In the subsequent years there has been a considerable amount of tree growth, as can be seen as 'Pacer' No 142009, forming a Chester to Manchester service, nears the station on 5 June 2002. *PDS/JCH*

NORTHWICH, SANDBACH JUNCTION: The Cheshire Midland Railway, supported by the Manchester Sheffield & Lincolnshire Railway and the Great Northern Railway, built the line from Altrincham to Knutsford, then on 1 January 1863 came the opening of the extension to Northwich. Ten years later, Messrs Brunner and Mond started their business in the nearby grounds of Winnington Hall, the forerunner of ICI. Although the LNWR had shown no interest in the line, in November 1867 it opened a branch line from Sandbach to Northwich via Middlewich, used first for freight and the following year for passenger services. This line joined the Northwich to Chester line at Sandbach Junction, just to the west of Northwich station. On 24 August 1973 English Electric Type 4 No 202 approaches Sandbach Junction signal box from the Chester direction hauling 'Covhops' loaded with soda ash, destined for one of the Yorkshire glass factories. The line to Middlewich and Sandbach goes off to the left.

On 5 June 2002 Class 37 No 37797 heads towards Chester hauling a short train of caustic soda tanks from Folly Lane to Warrington Arpley, destined for Dalry in Ayrshire. This service uses Northwich sidings to run round because there is no direct route between the Folly Lane branch and Warrington. *Tom Heavyside/JCH*

NORTHWICH station was opened by the Cheshire Midland Railway (later to become part of the CLC) in 1863. In this undated photograph looking east, we see a brake-van in the bay on the left-hand side, a water column at the platform end, occupied sidings, an array of semaphore signals, a signal box and ex-LNER 'J10' No 65160 (a long-standing Heaton Mersey engine) with a 4-4-0 'D10' or 'D11' beyond it, by the loco shed, which is just off the picture to the right.

There used to be a considerable amount of freight traffic, partly generated by Brunner Mond (later ICI), and although today there is still limestone traffic from Tunstead to the Brunner Mond works at Lostock and Oakleigh, the track layout at Northwich has been greatly simplified. On 5 June 2002 the remaining freight line is occupied by Class 37 No 37797. *Jim Peden collection/JCH*

NORTHWICH SHED was opened as a two-road shed by the West Cheshire Railway in 1869, and enlarged to four roads in 1876. It closed to steam in 1968, but continued in use as a diesel depot until 1984, before being demolished in 1991. At the end of 1947 the allocation consisted of 29 LNER engines, made up of three 'D10' 'Directors' for passenger work, 19 'J10' 0-6-0s primarily for freight use, one 'J11', four 'N5' tank engines and two 'L3' 2-6-4Ts. The shed also became home for the ex-LMS '8F' 2-8-0 'Consols', which hauled the ICI limestone hopper trains from Buxton to Northwich; there were over 20 of these locomotives allocated there at one time. In the diesel era the shed retained its link with the limestone trains, by then hauled mainly by Class 25s and 40s. On the date of the 'past' photograph, Boxing Day 1974, the depot contained two Class 08s, five Class 25s and three Class 40s

The area has since been redeveloped as a housing estate, now hidden from the railway by a line of trees, as seen on 19 August 2002. *Both JCH*

Around Altrincham

KNUTSFORD: The present station was opened in 1863 by the CLC, replacing the first one that had been opened by the Cheshire Midland only the previous year, following the extension of the line to Northwich. Comparison between the Edwardian postcard scene, looking towards Manchester, and the 'present' photograph, taken on 7 September 2002, shows that the substantial building on the right remains, although the platform canopy has been removed and the water tower demolished. The signal box at the north end of the Chester platform, known as Knutsford East, remained in excellent condition for some years after its closure, but was burned down by vandals in 1994. The station has undergone refurbishment and modernisation, particularly on the 'town' side. *Basil Jeuda collection/JCH*

MOBBERLEY: On the CLC line between Altrincham and Northwich, opened by the Cheshire Midland in 1862, Mobberley station is rather a long way from the village after which it is named. On 6 July 1965 Class '8F' 2-8-0 No 48676 passes the signal box with a consist of four-wheel covered wagons, only three years before the end of steam on British Railways. The shed plate is missing and '8L' has been painted on the front of the boiler, indicating allocation to Aintree shed.

The station building has had some modification and is now used as offices, and the semaphores have gone, but the box remains to control the road crossing. Class 142 No 142009 approaches with a Chester to Manchester service on 8 June 2002. *N. R. Knight/JCH*

HALE (1): A nearby pub called the 'Cheshire Midland' commemorates the line's opening by that company in 1862. Hale station was originally called Bowdon Peel Causeway, but this was shortened in 1899 to Peel Causeway before the name Hale was finally applied in 1902. In 1952 0-6-0 'J10' No 65171 (dating back to the latter part of the 19th century!), allocated to Northwich, storms through the station with a southbound mixed freight.

Today there are just two tracks through the station and the semaphores have been replaced by colour light signals operated from Deansgate Junction. On 8 June 2002 Class 153 No 153324, based at Newton Heath depot, forms a service from Chester to Manchester via Stockport. *Both JCH*

HALE (2): The limestone trains from Tunstead to Lostock and Oakleigh have long been a feature of the Altrincham to Northwich line. After the retirement of the LMS 2-8-0s, the trains saw a variety of diesel haulage including Classes 20, 25, 37, 47 and 60. In the photograph dated 10 June 1984 Class 47 No 47199 brings the 0955 Oakleigh to Tunstead empties over the level crossing.

The signal box closed in 1991 but remains in situ, as seen in the 'present' picture taken on 20 August 2002, as units Nos 158750 and 156429 arrive with the 0926 service from Northwich to Blackpool North. *PDS/JCH*

ALTRINCHAM (1): Class 304 electric unit No 304011, forming the 0618 service from Stockport, passes Altrincham North signal box before terminating at the station just beyond on 11 July 1989. When Metrolink was planned, the decision to have Altrincham as the southern terminus brought many changes. The signal box disappeared, the tracks approaching the station were doubled and the Metrolink trams were kept quite separate from the BR passenger and freight trains. The two tracks to the right in the view taken on 31 May 2002 are dedicated to trams, whereas the two tracks on the left are used by First North Western services from Manchester Piccadilly to Chester via Stockport and by freight traffic. *Both JCH*

ALTRINCHAM (2): Long before any thoughts of Metrolink, the station was the terminus of the Manchester South Junction & Altrincham Railway. The original facility of 1849 gave way to the present Altrincham & Bowdon station in 1881, shared with the CLC for its service to Northwich and Chester. In the photograph dated 8 August 1953, ex-GCR 4-4-0 'D10' No 62659 *Worsley-Taylor*, allocated to Northwich, approaches the station with the 12.35pm (Sat) Manchester-Northwich.

Today there is very little to link the two pictures; the signal box has gone, as have the lines to the right. On 8 June 2002 a Metrolink tram is leaving for Piccadilly. *H. C. Casserley/JCH*

ALTRINCHAM (3): In 1931 the MSJ&A line from Altrincham to Manchester was electrified by the LMS, current being supplied on the overhead system at 1,500 volts DC. The units were painted bright green and they remained in use until 1971 when the system was converted to the 25kv AC system, enabling trains to run through from Alderley Edge to Altrincham via the through platforms at Manchester Piccadilly. On 12 March 1966 a three-car unit headed by car M29235M arrives from Manchester.

At Altrincham the LMS units used two specific platforms, as do the Metrolink trams today; on 8 June 2002 tram No 1009 departs for Piccadilly. Although a new building has appeared to the left, the canopy supports are the same! Passengers using the Metro are warned that they must be in possession of a valid ticket before embarking on a tram. *D. L. Chatfield/JCH*

ALTRINCHAM (4): To the west of the station was the depot and stabling point for the LMS electrics. In the view from 31 March 1963 a unit headed by car No M29245 is about to enter the station, which can just be seen under the bridge arch, by Altrincham South signal box.

The change to the 'present' picture of 21 August 2002 is quite remarkable. The area where the depot and sidings were situated has been completely redeveloped, mainly with rather tasteful blocks of flats. The only point of reference is the road overbridge at the far end of the picture between the new buildings. The Metrolink trams terminate in the station before reaching the bridge. *D. L. Chatfield/JCH*

ALTRINCHAM (5): This turn-of-the-century postcard shows two open horse-drawn cabs lined up outside the station, while in the right-hand corner a horse-drawn omnibus can just be seen.

The small building just inside the station approach, most likely a cabmen's shelter, has gone today, but the clock tower remains much the same in the view of 21 August 2002. A bus station has been built in front of the station building, so it is now a three-way interchange between Metrolink trams, the Manchester to Chester rail service, and buses to a variety of destinations. *Mike Hitches collection/JCH*

NAVIGATION ROAD is the first station out of Altrincham in the Manchester direction. Originally an MSJ&A station dating from 1931, it became part of the Metrolink tram system when it opened in 1992. Class 37 No 6923 (37223) heads a southbound freight in the late 1960s as it approaches the station.

Following the opening of the Metrolink, the two tracks became quite separate – that on the left is dedicated to Metrolink, and that on the right is the Network Rail line for use by passenger trains from Manchester to Chester via Stockport, as well as freight traffic. Class 60 No 60061 approaches with train 6F06, comprising 25 Brunner Mond JEA limestone hopper wagons from Tunstead to Oakleigh, on 21 August 2002. *Keith Sanders/JCH*

Stockport area: LNWR lines

STOCKPORT EDGELEY STATION (1): Opened by the Manchester & Birmingham Railway in 1843 as just 'Stockport', the station soon acquired its 'Edgeley' suffix to avoid confusion with Tiviot Dale station. Situated at the south end of a large viaduct that carries the railway across the River Mersey, the station is some way from the centre of the town and has undergone a number of makeovers, including electrification and subsequent track rationalisation. On 9 April 1960 we see ex-LMS 2-6-4T No 42189 standing in one of the central roads with a three-coach train.

In the 'present' picture of 1 September 2002, both middle roads have gone, most of the chimneys have been removed from the building and the platform canopy has been modernised. Two-car Class 158 No 158776, in Northern Spirit Trans-Pennine livery, forms the 1451 Manchester Airport to Cleethorpes (via Piccadilly) service. *Michael Mensing/JCH*

STOCKPORT VIADUCT was opened in 1839 and is a great memorial to the 19th-century railway builders. Spanning the River Mersey, it is approximately one-third of a mile in length, and 111 feet high from the bed of the river to the parapet. In the photograph dated circa 1908, an LNWR loco crosses the viaduct with a southbound train.

The scene today has changed very little, although there is a new building on the right-hand side of the river, as photographed on 12 July 2002 with a two-car DMU heading south. *Courtesy Heritage Library, Stockport MBC/JCH*

STOCKPORT EDGELEY STATION (2): Looking south on 4 August 1968, the last day of steam, very clean-looking ex-LMS Class 5 4-6-0 No 45156 is at the head of a special to Carnforth, run by Stockport (Bahamas) Locomotive Society. We can see all the gantries and wires of the electrification of the line from Manchester to Crewe, which took place in 1960.

On the rather misty morning of 12 September 2002, the 'present' picture shows that the centre roads have been removed. Class 87 No 87034 *William Shakespeare* is at the 'country end' of a Euston-Manchester Piccadilly service. It is usual for these trains to be propelled on the up journey with a non-powered driving vehicle leading. *Hugh Ballantyne/JCH*

STOCKPORT EDGELEY SHED: Opened by the LNWR in 1883, situated south of the station and sandwiched between Stockport County FC's ground and the main line, Edgeley shed consisted of eight dead-end roads, with a multi-pitched roof installed in 1932. The shed closed in 1968 and was subsequently demolished. The first picture, dated 25 April 1951, shows ex-LNWR 0-6-0 'Cauliflower' No 58427, an ex-L&Y Aspinall 0-6-0, and several passenger tank engines.

The second photograph, taken on 30 March 1968, shows two members of Edgeley's then dwindling steam allocation, Class 5 No 44855 and 2-8-0 '8F' No 48549, together with a Class 24 diesel representing the new order.

After the building was demolished, the area remained undeveloped for many years. However, as seen in the third view from 15 July 2002, it is now home to the newly built Manchester South signalling centre, due to open in 2002/3, which will see the closure of six signal boxes between Cheadle Hulme and Heaton Norris Junction. The buildings to the left and rear provide the only visual link between 'past' and 'present'.
H. C. Casserley/Tom Heavyside/JCH

HAZEL GROVE, on the line from Stockport to Buxton, was opened in 1857 by the Stockport, Disley & Whaley Bridge Railway, later absorbed by the LNWR. Our Edwardian photograph shows a quiet country station, looking towards Stockport.

Today 'the Grove' has become a busy built-up area on the A6. The line from Stockport was electrified in 1981, and in 1986 a chord was put in from just east of the station, joining with the line from Northenden Junction to New Mills South Junction, enabling services from Manchester to the east of England to be routed via Stockport. At the time of electrification the station was completely modernised. However, as seen in the 'present' picture taken on 1 September 2002, the platform-mounted signal box dating from 1877 remains and the footbridge beyond the lattice one in the old photograph can just be seen. Class 170 unit No 170638, operated by Central Trains, approaches the station with a through service from Manchester to Norwich via the chord line. *Basil Jeuda collection/JCH*

CHEADLE HULME (1): The station on the present site was opened by the Manchester & Birmingham Railway in 1845, replacing the original station of 1842 located slightly further south. The relocation was necessary to accommodate the line to Macclesfield, which opened in 1845. The station name was initially Cheadle, but changed to Cheadle Hulme in 1866. In the 'past' picture, taken in 1958, we see an ex-LNWR 'G2A' Class 0-8-0 with an up freight on the Crewe line.

Electrification took place in 1960 to Crewe and 1967 to Stoke, and the whole junction was re-modelled in 2000. The signal box remains in situ, although it closed in 2001 as part of the major Stockport area re-signalling scheme. It was temporarily replaced by a portable building on the other side of the line, awaiting the opening of the new Manchester South Signalling Centre at Stockport. On 20 June 2002 First North Western Class 150 No 150143 takes the Macclesfield line with an empty stock working. The Macclesfield line is now the principal route for services from Manchester to Euston, Birmingham and beyond, with relatively few of these long-distance trains running via Crewe.

Martin Welch/JCH

CHEADLE HULME (2): Looking in the opposite direction, a four-coach train is pulling away towards Handforth in a photograph believed to have been taken around the turn of the 19th century. The line to Macclesfield is off to the left.

As can be seen in the 'present' picture of 20 June 2002, the platform buildings are now modern waiting shelters and the overall footbridge has gone (there now being no connection between the two outer and central platforms). Class 323 unit No 323227 is leaving with a Deansgate to Crewe service. *John Ryan collection/JCH*

WILMSLOW (1): Wilmslow station was opened by the Manchester & Birmingham Railway (later to become part of the LNWR) in 1842, on what was then the main line from Manchester to Crewe. Taken probably around the turn of the 19th century, the 'past' picture shows a line of horse-drawn cabs awaiting the arrival of a train. On the left is the goods yard with a board advertising Poynton & Worth Collieries; coal was brought in by private owner wagons and distributed by road locally. The goods yard could also deal with livestock and horses.

Today there is little evidence of the former station buildings but the narrow bridge on Station Road, under the railway, remains – albeit no longer cobbled! The goods yard, which finally closed in 1970, has given way to a much larger forecourt, and office accommodation has been built on the left, as seen in the 'present' picture taken on 17 June 2002. *Courtesy Wilmslow Historical Society/JCH*

WILMSLOW (2): In this view looking towards Crewe, taken probably around 1900, we see an LNWR train approaching on the down line. There is plenty of luggage on the platform, including some barrels, the contents of which are unknown. An advertisement for Finnigans department store, which after the Second World War moved to Wilmslow from Manchester, is on the up platform. The scene predates the opening of the Styal line in 1909, showing the goods yard and covered shed to the right where the Styal platforms would soon stand.

About 100 years later the chimneys of the platform building are clearly recognisable, but a subway has replaced the footbridge at the far end, and the supports and wires of electrification dominate the scene. On 17 June 2002 Class 158 No 158825, operated by Wales & Borders, calls with the 1533 service from Manchester Piccadilly to Cardiff, while on the right a Class 323 has just arrived forming the 1546 stopping service from Manchester Airport to Crewe. *Courtesy Cheshire & Chester Archives and Local Studies/JCH*

ALDERLEY EDGE: A relatively early comer in the history of railways, Alderley station was opened by the Manchester & Birmingham Railway in May 1842 on the main line from Crewe to Manchester London Road. It became Alderley & Chorley from 1853 to 1876, when it was renamed to the present title. The village has always attracted the affluent, from the days of the Manchester cotton merchants who commuted by train to Manchester to the current era with David Beckham and his wife having a home here. In earlier times it was a regular choice for picnics and excursions – it is reputed that on one day in June 1843 a train returning to Manchester 'carried over 3,000 passengers in 63 carriages'! On a postcard dated 1905 we see the station forecourt on the up side. The driver of the horse drawn carriage (wearing a 'boater') sits patiently, no doubt awaiting the arrival of a train, while to the right are several vans in the goods yard. Behind stands the Queen's Hotel, built and owned by the LNWR.

In today's view, taken on 1 June 2002, the station retains its original feel but close inspection reveals a number of changes: the lattice footbridge has been replaced by a concrete structure, the small station building has either been extended or replaced, the supports for the electrified line can be seen, and the hotel building has been converted into offices. The sports car completes the 21st-century scene. *John Ryan collection/JCH*

CHELFORD station was opened in 1842 on the Manchester to Crewe line between Alderley Edge and Goostrey, and has occasionally been referred to as Chelford for Knutsford. Just south of the station there are up and down loops. In the 'past' picture, ex-LMS 4-6-0 No 46150 *The Life Guardsman*, of Longsight shed, passes Chelford Loop signal box with a Manchester-bound express in the early 1950s.

The down loop can just be seen on the right-hand side beyond the trees as Class 158 unit No 158842, allocated to Cardiff Canton depot and operated by Wales & Borders, speeds through with a Cardiff to Manchester Piccadilly service on 25 September 2002. *Both JCH*

Stockport area: MR and CLC lines

CHEADLE HEATH station was opened by the Midland Railway in 1901 on its main line from Manchester to London via Derby; it had five through platform faces, each with a canopy. It was a busy suburban station and was also a stopping point for the Midland Pullman to and from London St Pancras. It closed to passengers in 1967 following the decision by British Railways to close the direct former Midland route between Derby and Manchester. Our 'past' picture shows immaculate-looking Midland Railway 'Flatiron' 0-6-4T No 2009 calling at the station with an up train.

Following closure, the station area was gradually redeveloped, and, as seen in the picture taken on 10 June 2002, all that remains is the single line running from Northenden Junction to Hazel Grove. There is no longer any passenger traffic through Cheadle Heath, but the regular Tunstead-Oakleigh limestone trains use the route. *R. M. Casserley collection/JCH*

HEATON MERSEY: Located between Stockport Tiviot Dale and Manchester Central, the station was opened by the Midland Railway in 1880. Until the line via Cheadle Heath was built, trains from Manchester Central to St Pancras used the route, calling at Tiviot Dale. In this postcard from the turn of the 19th century, postmarked Heaton Mersey, a Midland Railway 'Flatiron' tank engine pauses in the station.

Today nothing remains of the railway other than the name of the road from where the photograph was taken – Station Road. The whole station area has been redeveloped for housing, as seen in the 'present' picture taken on 13 September 2002. The Trans Pennine Trail pathway across the road uses part of the old trackbed. *John Ryan collection/JCH*

ROMILEY station was opened by the MS&LR in 1862. On 26 December 1952 – recalling the days when trains ran on Boxing Day – ex-LMS 4-4-0 Compound No 41103 of Leeds Holbeck shed enters the station with a service probably bound for Sheffield. The three starter signals represent, from left to right, the route to Skelton Junction via Stockport Tiviot Dale, the direct route to Manchester London Road via Reddish North, and the less direct route to London Road via Guide Bridge; note the practice of indicating the priority of routes by the relative height of each signal post. The photograph also shows a goods yard immediately to the right of the up platform, containing a number of two-axle wagons.

The goods yard closed in 1965 and the line to Tiviot Dale was axed in 1968. However, Romiley Junction signal box survived a local resignalling scheme and still adorns the 'present' photograph, dated 24 June 2002. A Class 142 DMU enters the station with a Manchester Piccadilly to Marple Rose Hill service. *C. H. A. Townley/JCH*

MARPLE station was opened in 1865 by the Sheffield & Midland Railway, replacing the temporary facility at Compstall for Marple upon the extension of the line across Goyt Cliff viaduct. On 30 May 1966 ex-LMS Class 5 4-6-0 No 45404 of Trafford Park shed awaits departure with the 3.30pm from Manchester Central to Sheffield Midland, while the 4.00pm Marple-Manchester Piccadilly diesel unit leaves on the down line.

The station is barely recognisable in the 'present' picture: the platform canopies have gone, as has the covered footbridge, and the island platform on the down side has been reduced to just one platform face. The day chosen to take the photograph, 10 September 2002, turned out to be one when First North Western drivers were on strike, so all was quiet at the station. *Ian Smith/JCH*

STRINES, GOYT CLIFF VIADUCT: Between the stations at Strines and Marple lies this handsome viaduct, carrying the railway over the valley of the River Goyt. Built in 1865 by the Manchester, Sheffield & Lincolnshire Railway (Sheffield & Midland Joint), the line forms a through route from Manchester into Derbyshire and on to Sheffield via the Hope Valley. On 19 June 1965 a Class 25 crosses the viaduct with the 5.30pm from Sheffield Midland to Manchester London Road.

With nearly 40 years of tree growth, access has become difficult, but almost the same view is still just possible, as seen on 13 June 2002, with a DMU forming the 1402 service from New Mills Central to Manchester Piccadilly. *Michael Mensing/JCH*

Stockport Tiviot Dale to Warrington

STOCKPORT TIVIOT DALE station was opened in 1865 by the Stockport, Timperley & Altrincham Junction Railway, later to become part of the CLC. The original spelling 'Teviot' hints at a connection with the Border country much further north. There were four lines through the station, plus bays at the east end. There was a small two-road loco shed on the north side of the line close to the station, which opened in 1866 and closed in 1889 when Heaton Mersey shed was commissioned. The Midland Railway used the station for its Manchester to St Pancras trains, until Cheadle Heath station was opened. Other passenger services ran to Liverpool Central. While the CLC did not have its own locomotives, it did have four Sentinel steam railcars, built in 1929, and for a period these worked between Stockport and Altrincham. This photograph shows the imposing but rather run-down frontage to the station, situated on the town side of the line with an entrance near the bottom of Lancashire Hill. *Courtesy Heritage Library Stockport MBC*

Opposite The 'past' view shows Tiviot Dale on 13 March 1965, looking east, only two years or so before passenger services ended and the station was closed. Ex-LMS Fowler 2-6-4T No 42343 of Edgeley shed enters the station on one of the through roads with a five-coach railtour, 'The Staffordshire Potter'.

Freight traffic continued until 1980, when the line was closed, supposedly temporarily, due to M63 construction work. In fact it never re-opened, and the road subsequently became part of the M60 Manchester outer ring road, as seen on 12 July 2002. *Gavin Morrison/JCH*

STOCKPORT CLUBHOUSE SIDINGS: After the closure of Tiviot Dale station in 1967, the former CLC line through Stockport remained a busy freight corridor for well over a decade. On 30 June 1976 Class 40 No 40025 heads a westbound coal train, having just passed George's Road signal box. The Class 40 would almost certainly have taken over from a Class 76 electric at Godley Junction. In the background, the viaduct carrying the Manchester to Crewe line can clearly be seen.

The second picture shows the trackless railway alignment on 24 January 1986, while the 'present' view, taken on 12 July 2002, shows that the CLC line has now completely disappeared and the whole area has been redeveloped. Several of the buildings on the skyline beyond the viaduct remain, although the cooling tower has been demolished. *Tom Heavyside/JCH (2)*

Opposite NORTHENDEN JUNCTION (1): For many years the CLC line between Northenden Junction and Skelton Junction was a busy bottleneck, with several routes converging at each end. Class 47 No 47182 approaches Northenden Junction from the Cheadle North direction with 6M53, a loaded merry-go-round coal train from Wath to Fiddlers Ferry power station, on 10 June 1975. At that time there were no fewer than 11 scheduled coal trains each weekday from South Yorkshire to Fiddlers Ferry, all routed via Woodhead and the CLC line to Warrington.

In 1989 the line between Hazel Grove and Northenden via Cheadle North was singled and the junction was remodelled, as can be seen in the 'present' picture dated 16 August 2002. A Freightliner Class 66/5 passes the junction with empty cement wagons for Hope (Earles Sidings). The siding on the right serves one of Manchester's four rail-served refuse transfer stations, dispatching containerised refuse to Roxby landfill site in Lincolnshire. *Both JCH*

NORTHENDEN JUNCTION (2): A few hundred yards to the west of the signal box, on the down side of the line, close to where the CLC station was situated, a cement terminal was opened on the site of the old goods yard, which had been closed in 1965. The operator was originally the Associated Portland Cement Company, later to become Blue Circle Cement. Loaded cement tanks arrived from Earles Sidings, the wagons were propelled into the siding, the empties collected, then the loco and consist either ran to Skelton Junction, where the engine could run round before returning to Earles Sidings, or went on to Warrington as part of a wagonload service. The latter was the case on 15 May 1989, when Class 47/3 No 47322 was pictured shunting PCA cement tanks. The shunting manoeuvres had to be completed as quickly as possible to clear the line before the arrival of the next DMU with a Manchester to Chester service, routed via Stockport and the ex-LNWR line to Northenden Junction.

Following the opening of the cement terminal at Weaste in July 2000, Blue Circle withdrew from Northenden. A visit on 16 June 2002 found the former cement sidings gradually becoming overgrown, as Class 60 No 60092 arrived with the empty containers for Northenden refuse transfer station. In late 2002 the Strategic Rail Authority awarded Lafarge a Freight Facilities Grant to convert the sidings into a roadstone terminal. *PDS/JCH*

Opposite SKELTON JUNCTION (1): Looking west we see the triple junction: to the left is the line to Lymm and Warrington, in the centre that to Cadishead, and to the right one that, after the initial bend, turns to the left and goes underneath the other two, heading south to Northwich and beyond. In the photograph of 25 April 1968, a 'Consol' 2-8-0 is coming off the Lymm line with an empty coal train. At one time, in the open area to the right of the train, there were quite extensive sidings.

Today the signal box has gone, a single line remains to Partington (currently out of use) and the trees have obscured much of the line round to Deansgate Junction, as seen on 28 June 2002. A four-car set consisting of a Class 142 with No 150225 forms a Manchester Piccadilly to Chester service. *Roger Siviter/JCH*

SKELTON JUNCTION (2): Looking east, back towards the junction, a more modern-looking signal box has replaced the earlier structure as a loaded limestone train passes en route from Tunstead (near Buxton) to Oakleigh (near Northwich) on 11 June 1982, hauled by Class 40 No 40061 and Class 25 No 25306.

The signal box and semaphores went in 1991, and the modern gantry holds the equivalent colour light signals with 'feathers' – rows of white lights – above them. The 'V' indicates routes to the left, for the main line to Northenden Junction, and to the right for entry into a loop on the down side. 'Pacer' No 142029 passes with the 1424 Manchester Piccadilly to Chester service on 11 June 1982. *Both JCH*

DUNHAM MASSEY was located on the LNWR line (originally the St Helens Canal & Railway Company) from Skelton Junction to Warrington Bank Quay Low Level, and was opened in 1853 as Warburton, undergoing several name changes until acquiring its final title in 1861. Serving a very small local population, it closed just over a century later in 1962. Our 'past' picture, looking east, is taken from the level crossing and shows the simple station facilities on 10 April 1957.

The trackbed is now part of the Trans Pennine Trail, but some rails remain on the crossing and a telegraph post to the right of the finger-post has survived, as seen in the photograph taken on 5 June 2002. *H. C. Casserley/JCH*

HEATLEY & WARBURTON (1): The quite substantial station buildings at this relatively minor intermediate station are pictured on 10 April 1957.

Subsequently the signal box and footbridge have been demolished and the trees have grown up, but most of the buildings remain, including part of the station, as seen in the 'present' picture taken on 5 June 2002. The Trans Pennine Trail stretches from Liverpool to Hull, for the use of walkers, cyclists and horse riders. *H. C. Casserley/JCH*

CONGLETON: Opened by the North Staffordshire Railway in 1848, Congleton station, on the Manchester to Stoke main line, is almost a mile from the town centre. In the view of 1962 it appears that the down platform is being re-built. We can see the original station buildings, the signal box and crossing gates; there is also a goods yard to the right and a bay to the left of the up platform.

Later a road overbridge was built at the south end, with the subsequent abolition of the crossing. The goods yard is now closed, although the main building remains in use by a private firm. The bay has gone and the buildings have been replaced by a less than attractive pre-fabricated structure. The line was electrified in 1967, so the overhead wires dominate in the view of 25 September 2002, as a Virgin 'Voyager' speeds south with a Cross Country service from Manchester. In the summer timetable of 2002, there were six down trains stopping between 0700 and 0930, but then only one stopping service through the day until 1643. However, after September 2002 there was a great improvement with a number of Virgin Cross Country services calling. *Martin Welch collection/JCH*

NORTH RODE: Located between Macclesfield and Congleton and opened in 1849, this North Staffordshire station was originally known as North Rode Junction, because of the line to Leek that left the main line just south of the station. In about 1955 rebuilt 'Royal Scot' 4-6-0 No 46131 *The Royal Warwickshire Regiment*, allocated to Longsight shed, is at the head of a Manchester London Road to Euston express. As can be seen, there was a substantial station house.

Nothing remains today but the double-track main line, as a Class 86 heads the 1536 Manchester Piccadilly to Birmingham International service on 27 June 2002. *Frank Wemyss-Smith, courtesy Martin Welch/JCH*

MACCLESFIELD CENTRAL (1): Jointly opened in 1873 by the Manchester, Sheffield & Lincolnshire and North Staffordshire companies, Macclesfield Central was the terminus of what became the GCR/LNER line from Manchester to Macclesfield via Marple Rose Hill, and was to become the town's only station when Hibel Road closed in 1960. Hibel Road was in a very tight geographical position and Central had more space for development. Ex-LMS

'Jubilee' 4-6-0 No 45601 *British Guiana*, allocated to Camden shed (1B), passes through with the 12.05pm Manchester London Road to Euston express in 1958.

The Manchester to Stoke line was electrified in 1967 and the station was modernised, with a down platform on the town side of the line, and an island platform for the up main on one side and a bi-directional line on the other used mainly for local trains to Manchester. There is no railway link with the photograph of 15 July 2002, although the mill building behind remains as a Manchester Piccadilly to Euston train prepares to stop, headed by an unpowered driving vehicle with an electric loco propelling at the rear. *Martin Welch/JCH*

103

MACCLESFIELD CENTRAL (2): In this track-level view of the station, dated 18 April 1954, we see the relative simplicity of the station with its through roads, signal box at the Manchester end on the down side, and a fine array of semaphore signals.

Since the completion of the Silk Road town bypass, the only view from the east side of the line is looking down on the station. On 1 June 2002 a new Virgin 'Voyager' Class 220 stops with a Cross Country service. *H. C. Casserley/JCH*

MACCLESFIELD HIBEL ROAD replaced the first station on the Manchester & Birmingham Railway, named Beech Road, in 1849. It was the main-line station for the town until 1960, when it closed in favour of the ex-GCR/NSR Central station. Ex-LMS rebuilt 'Patriot' 4-6-0 No 45523 *Bangor*, from Camden shed, leaves Hibel Road Tunnel at the head of a Manchester London Road to Euston train around 1954. To the right can just be seen the turntable pit leading to the three-road ex-NSR loco shed, which survived as a signing-on point until 1965.

Little remains of the station today, as seen in the picture taken on 15 July 2002. A Virgin Class 220 'Voyager' approaches the station with the 1015 from Manchester Piccadilly to Birmingham New Street service. The cottages up on the left and those above the tunnel mouth provide the link between the two pictures. *Martin Welch/JCH*

PRESTBURY: The line from Cheadle Hulme to Macclesfield was opened by the Manchester & Birmingham Railway in 1845, subsequently becoming part of the LNWR. At that time Prestbury must have been a tiny hamlet, but later it became a favourite home for wealthy commuters to Manchester, and today the village is one of the most attractive in the county. Our 'past' picture was taken in the mid-1950s and shows Caprotti Class 5 4-6-0 No 44750, allocated to Longsight shed, at the head of a Manchester-bound express.

Following electrification in 1967 the line grew in importance and is now considered the principal route from Manchester to the south, joining the Crewe-Euston line at Colwich Junction. The station shows remarkably little sign of change – the lattice footbridge has given way to one of concrete, the semaphore signals have been replaced by colour lights, and of course the infrastructure of electrification is prominent. Three-car Class 323 unit No 323237 arrives with a stopping train from Stoke to Manchester Piccadilly on 1 June 2002. *Stations UK/JCH*

POYNTON: The present station opened in 1887, replacing the earlier station at Poynton Midway (1845-1887). The line passed close to the various Poynton collieries, and coal was sent out from the goods yard by the station. There was a substantial station house on the up side, as seen in the picture taken around 1900.

In the current photograph, taken on 1 June 2002, electrification supports and wires dominate the scene, the footbridge has been replaced and the signal box is a distant memory, having closed in 1963. A Manchester Piccadilly to Euston express is entering the station, with an unpowered driving vehicle at the head and an electric loco propelling from the rear. *John Ryan collection/JCH*

BOLLINGTON was the last station before Macclesfield on the ex-GCR/LNER line from Manchester, serving a quite large community. Opened in 1869 by the Macclesfield, Bollington & Marple Railway, it survived for just over a century until closure in 1970. In the last few days of operation, a two-car Birmingham RC&W unit (later Class 104) is pictured leaving the station heading towards Macclesfield. The brick-built station buildings were substantial, and at one time the location handled considerable goods traffic, including raw cotton and coal for local textile firms.

Adelphi Mill, behind the station, remains in use today, together with other buildings seen in the photograph of 27 June 2002. The trackbed for a large part is now the Middlewood Way, offering a very pleasant walk through the Cheshire countryside. *Martin Welch/JCH*

HIGHER POYNTON: Located between High Lane and Bollington, Higher Poynton station was opened in 1869 as Poynton, which was rather optimistic as it was a long walk from Poynton village! Its name was changed to Higher Poynton (with the suffix 'for Lyme Park' added in some timetables) in 1930, and it remained so until closure in 1970. An ex-GCR 4-4-2T (LNER Class 'C13') is taking water at the head of a Macclesfield-bound train in May 1951.

In the view of 10 June 2002, the Manchester platform remains and the chimneys of the Boar's Head public house can be seen above the trees, but the rest of the station is now an attractive picnic spot on the Middlewood Way. *C. H. A. Townley/JCH*

MIDDLEWOOD HIGHER: Between High Lane and Higher Poynton on the Marple Rose Hill to Macclesfield line, Middlewood Higher station opened in 1879 and survived until 1970, when the line closed. It lay at right angles to Middlewood Lower station on the LNWR Hazel Grove to Buxton line, still open today. Both stations were isolated, with no public road access. Even today the only approach to the remaining ex-LNWR station, other than arriving by train, is from the Middlewood Way footpath and bridleway. In the first photograph, taken on 18 April 1954 from a Macclesfield-bound train, looking towards High Lane, we see the basic wooden platform and building.

Nothing survives today except the bridge over the Buxton line, still visible in the 'present' picture of 18 July 2002. *H. C. Casserley/JCH*

MIDDLEWOOD LOW LEVEL: In March 1952 ex-LNWR design 0-8-0 '7F' No 49081 (allocated to Widnes) heads a mixed goods round the curve from Middlewood Tunnel towards the Low Level station, passing the LNWR signal box. The train would have originated at Buxton, but the destination is unknown. The line in the foreground, behind the photographer, leads to the junction with high-level GCR/NSR line between Macclesfield Central and Romiley. Trains from the Macclesfield direction heading for Buxton used a flyover to reach the low level. The building behind the engine is believed to be a brick works.

Today the whole area of this interesting junction has been taken over by trees and scrub, with the exception of the remaining low-level line to Buxton, as seen in the 'present' picture taken from the east end of Middlewood Low Level station on 18 July 2002. *C. H. A. Townley/JCH*

HIGH LANE: With its origins in the 1864 incorporation of the Macclesfield, Bollington & Marple Railway, High Lane station was situated on the line from Marple Wharf Junction to Macclesfield Central. The station opened in 1869 and survived for 101 years before closure, which was pretty good going considering the very small local population throughout its life. The line was originally single track but was doubled in 1871, requiring the building of second platforms at the intermediate stations. On 26 April 1966 a DMU calls with a Manchester London Road to Macclesfield Central service.

Following the line closure the trackbed was made into a walking and cycling route known as the Middlewood Way, which was officially opened in 1985. Little of the former station remains, but the brick platform base can be seen in the 'present' photograph taken on 20 June 2002. *Martin Welch/JCH*

Crewe and district

BEESTON CASTLE & TARPORLEY was one of five intermediate stations between Crewe and Chester. Opened in 1842 by the LNWR as Beeston, its name was changed to Beeston Castle in 1868 and the suffix '& Tarporley' was added in 1873. There was very little population near the station – the village of Tarporley was a good 2 miles away – but passenger trains nonetheless continued to call until 1966. This view of the station entrance on the down side, taken on 29 August 1964, shows the quite substantial building, of which nothing now remains, as seen in the 'present' picture of 6 August 2002.

The third picture, dated 22 August 1964, shows Class 5 4-6-0 No 45276 passing through the station with a Llandudno to Nottingham train. Just above the last coaches is the signal box, dating back to 1914, which remains in use today. *H. C. Casserley/JCH/R. M. Casserley*

CREWE NORTH SHED was a complex site comprising a brick-built four-road shed and a 12-road dead-end shed side by side, situated on the down side of the line just north of Crewe station. An adjacent semi-roundhouse with eight tracks was added after the Second World War. It was a Mecca for all engine-spotters and there cannot be many who did not attempt to 'bunk' round the shed when it was full of exciting top link locos, from the streamlined 'Princess Coronations' to 'Princess Royals', 'Royal Scots', 'Jubilees', etc. A footbridge connected the station with the shed and formed a wonderful spotting place when authority permitted. On 13 February 1965, only three years before the end of steam, ex-LMS re-built 'Royal Scot' 4-6-0 No 46115 *Scots Guardsman* (subsequently preserved) catches the early morning sunlight as it comes off shed to work the RCTS 'Farewell to Royal Scots' commemorative tour to Carlisle via Blackburn and the Settle & Carlisle line. The engine was allocated to Carlisle Kingmoor (12A).

The shed closed in 1965 and the site completely cleared. Today part of the site is empty, part is taken up by the modern Crewe Signalling Centre, and part is a car park, as seen on 30 September 2002. In the distance the chimneys of the Crewe Arms can just be seen in both photographs. *Hugh Ballantyne/JCH*

CREWE STATION (1): The station has undergone a number of changes, particularly in 1985 when there was a major rationalisation. On 27 September 1960 BR Standard 2-6-0 No 78037, with a 24K (Preston) shedplate, stands in one of the bays at the north end of the station with empty coaching stock.

Comparison with the 'present' picture, taken on 6 August 2002, shows that there has been very little visible change except that the platform numbers have changed: the one on which the photographer is standing was 4A and is now Platform 9. On 6 August 2002 First North Western Class 175 No 175113 has just arrived from North Wales and will form the 1010 return working to Bangor. *Michael Mensing/JCH*

CREWE STATION (2): The bays at the south end of the station on the down side have long been associated with
trains to Nantwich, Whitchurch, Shrewsbury and, until 1963, to Market Drayton and Wellington. Crewe had a
small GWR engine shed at Gresty Lane with an allocation of three or four locomotives. On 23 September 1961,
BR Standard 2-6-2T No 41232, allocated to Wellington shed, awaits departure with the 5.20pm to Wellington.

Today trains for the Central Wales line, stopping services to Shrewsbury and some of the longer-distance trains
to South Wales use the bay platforms. There is very little change to be seen in the surroundings in the photograph
taken on 6 August 2002, although there is a very different type of train. Class 153 No 153320 forms the 1027 to
Shrewsbury; the unit is operated by Wales & Borders in an orange livery, with a scenic picture on the side.

CREWE STATION (3): In this undated photograph, North Staffordshire Railway 4-4-2T No 14 is coming off the Chester line with a rake of 10 or more coaches, no doubt returning to the Potteries with an excursion from North Wales. To the left we see the old signal box at the junction of the Chester line and the main line to Scotland, and the curious overhead system that linked Crewe station with the locomotive works.

In the 'present' picture of 6 August 2002, a Class 175 'Coradia' unit is arriving from Chester. Behind it can be seen another old signal box, Crewe North Junction, which is now part of the Crewe Heritage Centre. *John Feild*

CREWE STATION (4): Looking north along the main line, in a photograph dating from about 1900, an LNWR 2-4-0 'Jumbo' has come off the Manchester line to the right. The Chester line branches off to the left by the signal box, and we can see the 'spider bridge' carrying the 18-inch track of the works tramway, used for bringing spare parts, etc, to the station for dispatch over the LNWR system. The signalman must have been waiting for the train to pass as the signal has immediately been returned to the horizontal.

There have been many changes, including some track rationalisation, but the basic three-way junction is the same. On 30 September 2002 EWS Class 66 No 66249 has crossed from the main line to the west side of the station with a long rake of new HTA coal hoppers. *Basil Jeuda collection/JCH*

The Woodhead route

GUIDE BRIDGE (1): The LNER reached Manchester by means of the former Manchester Sheffield & Lincolnshire/Great Central route via Woodhead Tunnel and Guide Bridge. Class 'J38' 0-6-0 No 5902 stands at Guide Bridge with an eastbound train on the morning of 15 September 1945. The list of places on the station nameboard gives an idea of the importance of Guide Bridge on the early railway map. The semaphore signals were unusual in being pneumatically operated.

Electrification transformed Guide Bridge in the 1950s, and in more recent times the platform lines have been reduced from four to two. The only passenger trains calling here today are the Manchester to Glossop/Hadfield locals, while freight declined sharply after the closure of the Woodhead route in 1981. Class 56 No 56099 is pictured passing Guide Bridge with a train of empty BDA steel carriers from the Stockport direction on 24 June 2002. *H. C. Casserley/JCH*

GUIDE BRIDGE (2): Ex-GCR Class 'O4' 2-8-0 No 63785, allocated to Retford, heads west past Guide Bridge East box on 13 June 1949. By this time work had already started on wiring up the Woodhead route for 1,500 volts DC operation, and the days of ex-GCR steam locomotives working across the Pennines to Manchester were numbered.

Track rationalisation has left Guide Bridge East box oddly set back from the remaining running lines. No 60077 approaches the station with 6M05, the 0930 empty refuse containers from Roxby to Northenden, on 24 June 2002. At the time of writing EWS operates three daily trainloads of household refuse from Greater Manchester transfer stations to Roxby landfill site near Scunthorpe. The overhead wires are used only by the Class 323 units on the Manchester to Glossop/Hadfield service. *H. C. Casserley/JCH*

HYDE NORTH station was built where the GCR/MR joint line to Romiley diverged from the GCR line from Manchester to Sheffield via Woodhead. Opened as Hyde Junction in 1863, it was renamed Hyde North in 1951. In our 'past' photograph of 18 April 1954, ex-GCR 4-4-2T No 67447 (a Gorton engine) arrives with the 9.28am (Sun) Manchester London Road to Macclesfield train.

As can be seen in the picture of 24 June 2002, a number of industrial buildings have been demolished, and a signal gantry has been added. The electrification gantry beyond must be the only one on the line to Marple Rose Hill, which is the destination of the Class 101 No 101692 approaching with a service from Manchester Piccadilly. *H. C. Casserley/JCH*

GLOSSOP: Barely 2 miles long, the Glossop branch was built in the 1840s by the Duke of Norfolk, a prominent local landowner, who wanted his own connection with the nascent Sheffield, Ashton-under-Lyne & Manchester Railway (SAMR). The SAMR soon took over the branch and in 1884 its successor, the Manchester Sheffield & Lincolnshire Railway, greatly enhanced it with double track and a triangular junction at Dinting. In 1954 British Railways introduced an all-electric service to Glossop, using eight three-car multiple units based on an earlier LNER design. Pictured at the terminus on 8 July 1983 are cars M59404M, M59504M and M59604M, then in their 30th year of service.

After closure of the Woodhead route, BR retained electric operation to Glossop and Hadfield but converted the power supply to 25kv AC to allow withdrawal of the by then elderly electric units. Representing the latest generation of suburban stock, unit No 323233 stands at Glossop with a Manchester to Hadfield working on 23 January 2002. *Both PDS*

TORSIDE: Realising a plan put forward by the LNER as long ago as 1926, British Railways completed the electrification of the Woodhead route in 1954. The main purpose of electrification was to handle more efficiently the huge volumes of coal and other freight requiring transport across the Pennines. The locomotive fleet comprised 57 EM1 (later Class 76) Bo-Bo electrics for freight and some passenger work, and seven EM2 Co-Co locomotives for express passenger duties. In later years many of the Class 76s were equipped with train air brakes and multiple working equipment, enabling them to haul 'merry-go-round' and container trains. Nos 76021 and 76026 pass Torside with a westbound Freightliner service on 16 June 1981.

The trackbed between Hadfield and Woodhead now forms the Longdendale Trail, part of the Trans Pennine Trail that runs from Liverpool to Hull for the benefit of walkers, cyclists and horse-riders. The 'present' photographs are dated 23 January 2002. *All PDS*

WOODHEAD (1): The station at the remote outpost of Woodhead can never have generated much traffic and its closure in 1964 came as no surprise. Class 76 No 76035 passes the disused station platforms with 8E46, the 0730 Warrington Arpley to Tinsley wagonload service, on 18 June 1981. The wires were extended to Tinsley yard in 1965 to allow through electric operation, but this train – like many others – would still have required a change from diesel to electric traction at Godley Junction.

The need for most trains to change locomotives en route was one reason why the Woodhead route closed in 1981, after just 27 years of electric operation. Traces of the westbound platform are still visible in the 'present' photograph dated 23 January 2002. *Both PDS*

WOODHEAD (2): Class 76 No 76051 sets back on to the westbound line before entering the 'new' Woodhead tunnel with an eastbound train of MCO mineral wagons on 22 August 1980; the wrong line working was because of repairs on the eastbound track in the tunnel. The double-track tunnel had opened in 1954 to replace the two original single-track bores, of which the linings had deteriorated alarmingly after a century of steam operation. The Central Electricity Generating Board took over the old tunnel bores to carry power lines across the Pennines with minimal environmental disruption.

Most of the railway buildings at Woodhead have disappeared since closure of the line, but the infrastructure of the electricity supply industry remains prominent. The trackbed is pictured on 25 April 2002. *JCH/PDS*

DUNFORD BRIDGE station marked the east end of Woodhead Tunnel. Despite the lack of habitation nearby it remained open to goods until 1963 and to passengers until 1970. LNER 'K3' 2-6-0 No 112 (later to become British Railways No 61912) approaches Dunford Bridge with a westbound mixed goods train on the afternoon of 15 September 1945.

The tracks through Dunford Bridge were realigned for the opening of the new Woodhead Tunnel in 1954. Class 76 locos Nos 76039 and 76037 haul 8M29, the 0325 Mansfield Concentration Sidings to Garston Dock coal train, over the 'new' alignment on 8 January 1981. The old trackbed can be seen between the signal box and the leading locomotive.

Both old and new railway alignments have now passed into history. Today the trackbed between Dunford Bridge and Penistone forms part of the Upper Don Trail. *H. C. Casserley/PDS*

INDEX OF LOCATIONS